TOUCHING THE LIGHT OF DAY:
SIX URUGUAYAN POETS

TOUCHING THE LIGHT OF DAY:
SIX URUGUAYAN POETS

Selection and translations
by Laura Chalar

With introductions by Gerardo Ferreira

velizbooks.com

For further information write Veliz Books:
P.O. Box 920243, El Paso, TX 79912
velizbooks.com

ISBN 978-0-9969134-2-3

Cover image, "Muñeca escapada,"
and illustrations by Raquel Barboza.
All rights reserved.

Cover design by Silvana Ayala.

To Filomena and Catalina

But I sometimes touched the light of day.

Líber Falco

CONTENTS

A NOTE ON THE SELECTION

This is a purely personal selection, drawn from the work of some but by no means all of the many Uruguayan poets I have read, enjoyed, and been transformed by over the last few years.

As such, it does not claim to be, nor should it be viewed as, in any way representative of Uruguayan poetry in general or any school or style within it.

I hope it will, however, provide the interested reader with a glimpse of the rich panorama of our literature (and, indirectly, of our country), making him or her keen to find out more. If I can introduce even one such reader to these haunting poems and to Uruguay's poetry tradition, I shall consider the selection successful.

My selection covers authors whose poems are in the public domain.

Laura Chalar

Julio Herrera y Reissig

A SCULPTOR OF WORDS:
JULIO HERRERA Y REISSIG

Julio Herrera y Reissig (Montevideo, 1875-1910) was a part of the Uruguayan so-called "1900s Generation." This was a group of writers who cultivated different genres (drama, poetry, essay, and fiction), shared "the same spiritual and cultural climate in turn-of-the-century Uruguay, and produced their works between 1895 and 1925" (Mirza 15). Alongside that of Herrera y Reissig, we find names such as Roberto de las Carreras, Delmira Agustini, Horacio Quiroga, José Enrique Rodó, Carlos Vaz Ferreira, and Florencio Sánchez—all of them relevant to any literary analysis of that time, both for their cultural and historical importance and for their individual output, notwithstanding the fact that each had his or her own career and that their life experiences, as may be expected, were very different.

Back in those times, the prevailing aesthetics were those of Modernist sensibilities, a renewing trend of which Herrera y Reissig was the great local exponent, following in and enhancing the local footsteps of José Martí, Rubén Darío, and Leopoldo Lugones. This is not the place to explore the multiple stylistic expressions of this movement, or its features and specificities—or to list the number of resources which Herrera himself contributed to Modernism and capitalized with his copious, intense, elegant and erudite pen.[1]

The early trace left by English Romanticism in his thoughts soon gave way to the astonishment and interest aroused by late nineteenth-century French poetry, Parnassianism and Symbolism, trends that merge and mix in his poetry—a poetry difficult to penetrate without a constellation map to guide travelers. This is a poetic universe conceived not only through creative will—the formal (linguistic, phonetic, and metric) richness of Herrera's works demonstrates his tireless striving towards perfection, which lies at the very core of his verse. In Herrera's poems, imagination and emotion drive each other and engage in an intimate dialogue, condensed in the close correspondence between the musical value of words and their plastic/evocative sense (the latter criticized by some for allegedly being too exuberant or excessive). When reading Herrera's sonnets, one cannot help feeling that he is a sculptor of words, for every verse appears to have been chiseled until the perfect form was achieved.

A congenital heart disease dogged him from his youth and up to his last days; to this, there was added the contagion of a typhoid fever that sealed his fate. His delicate condition required him to resort to morphine, a practice that gave rise to extravagant opinions on his dandyism, an attitude or pose he cultivated more *pour la galerie* than from actual conviction. He founded a very famous salon called the "Tower of the Panoramas," held in an attic of his family home and where he acted as host and promoted meetings between intellectuals and writers.[2]

Julio Herrera y Reissig was (and is) an essential writer in the scene of early twentieth-century Latin American poetry. He was barely thirty five years old when he died without having ever published a book, but leaving a legacy capable of making us all forget death.[3]

NOTES

[1] For a more comprehensive study of the works of Herrera y Reissig, we refer the reader to *Poesía completa y prosas. Julio Herrera y Reissig*, a critical edition coordinated by Ángeles Estévez, 2nd edition, Madrid, Galaxia Gutenberg, 1999. From the author's works we especially recommend *Los éxtasis de la montaña* (1907), *Los parques abandonados* (1908), and *La torre de las esfinges* (1909), among others.

[2] "Built between 1850 and 1875, [the house] has two floors, originally designed for family dwelling. Formerly the home of Julio Herrera y Reissig, it was declared National Heritage in 1975. It was remodeled in the early twentieth century, when Art Déco ornaments were added to its façade. In the 1980s it was restored, and it is now the seat of the National Academy of Letters of the Ministry of Education and Culture. Its façade boasts a wrought-iron balcony and the lookout [attic]. Its state of repair is average, especially on the inside. The façade is in need of maintenance." Source: *Inventario del patrimonio arquitectónico y urbanístico de la Ciudad Vieja*, available at bit.ly/1MLNaNu.

[3] The year 2006 saw the first-ever edition of *Tratado de la imbecilidad del país por el sistema de Herbert Spencer*, written by Herrera y Reissig between 1900 and 1902, thanks to the research of scholar Aldo Mazzucchelli, who writes in his introduction: "The gathering, deciphering, ordering, and publishing of these manuscripts, over a hundred years later, enables the complete [...] placement and explanation of the close consistency between two issues that hitherto seemed separated: on the one side, the isolation vis-à-vis the hegemonic values of society, which Herrera y Reissig experienced both intellectually and socially during his short life; and, on the other side, the isolation in which the mainstream criticism held this prose work [...], segregating it from the rest of Herrera's works and actually quarantining these defiant writings."

EL DESPERTAR

Alisia y Cloris abren de par en par la puerta
y torpes, con el dorso de la mano haragana,
restréganse los húmedos ojos de lumbre incierta
por donde huyen los últimos sueños de la mañana.

La inocencia del día se lava en la fontana,
el arado en el surco vagaroso despierta
y en torno a la casa rectoral, la sotana
del cura se pasea gravemente en la huerta…

Todo suspira y ríe. La placidez remota
de la montaña sueña celestiales rutinas.
El esquilón repite siempre su misma nota

de grillo de las cándidas églogas matutinas.
Y hacia la aurora sesgan agudas golondrinas
como flechas perdidas de la noche en derrota.

THE AWAKENING

Alysia and Chloris open the door wide
and clumsily, with the back of a lazy hand,
rub their moist eyes filled with uncertain light,
across which the morning's last dreams are fleeing.

The innocence of day washes in the fountain,
the plow awakens in its torpid furrow
and, around the parsonage, the priest's
cassock gravely strolls the orchard…

Everything sighs and laughs. The mountain's remote
calmness dreams heavenly routines.
The cowbell repeats its unchanging note,

a cricket to the artless morning eclogues.
And towards dawn sharp swallows slant away,
like lost arrows of the defeated night.

LA VELADA

La cena ha terminado: legumbres, pan moreno
y uvas aún lujosas de virginal rocío…
Rezaron ya. La Luna nieva un candor sereno
y el lago se recoge con lácteo escalofrío.

El anciano ha concluido un episodio ameno
y el grupo desanúdase con un placer cabrío…
Entre tanto, allá fuera, en un silencio bueno,
los campos demacrados encanecen de frío.

Lux canta. Lidé corre. Palemón anda en zancos.
Todos ríen… La abuela demándales sosiego.
Anfión, el perro, inclina, junto al anciano ciego,

ojos de lazarillo, familiares y francos…
Y al son de las castañas que saltan en el fuego
palpitan al unísono sus corazones blancos.

EVENING

Dinner is over: vegetables, black bread and grapes
still lustrous with virginal dew… They have
prayed already. A calm candor falls snowlike from the Moon
and the lake retires with a milky shiver.

The old man has finished an amusing anecdote
and the group unknots with goatlike pleasure—
while out in the distance, in kindly silence,
the gaunt fields turn white with cold.

Lux sings. Lide runs. Palaemon walks on stilts.
They all laugh… Grandmother asks for quiet.
The family pet, Amphion, turns to the blind old man

a seeing-eye dog's familiar, frank gaze…
And to the sound of chestnuts leaping in the fire
their pure-white hearts beat all in unison.

EL CURA

Es el cura… Lo han visto las crestas silenciarias,
luchando de rodillas con todos los reveses,
salvar en pleno invierno los riesgos montañeses
o trasponer de noche las rutas solitarias.

De su mano propicia, que hace crecer las mieses,
saltan como sortijas gracias involuntarias;
y en su asno taumaturgo de indulgencias plenarias
hasta el umbral del cielo lleva a sus feligreses…

Él pasa del hisopo al zueco y la guadaña;
él ordeña la pródiga ubre de su montaña
para encender con oros el pobre altar de pino;

de sus sermones fluyen suspiros de albahaca;
el único pecado que tiene es un sobrino…
Y su piedad humilde lame como una vaca.

THE PRIEST

It's the priest... The silence-keeping summits have seen him
—struggling on his knees against all mishaps—
clear mountain risks in dead of winter
or cross in the night the lonely roads.

From his propitious hand that swells the harvests
leap like rings involuntary graces—
on a wonder-working donkey he carries his flock
to the gates of heaven by plenary indulgences...

He goes from the sprinkler to the clogs and scythe,
and milks his mountain's bountiful udders
to light up with gold the modest pinewood altar;

basil sighs flow from his sermons.
His only sin is a nephew...
And his humble piety licks like a cow.

LA NOCHE

La noche en la montaña mira con ojos viudos
de cierva sin amparo que vela ante su cría;
y como si asumieran un don de profecía
en un sueño inspirado hablan los campos rudos.

Rayan el panorama, como espectros agudos,
tres álamos en éxtasis… Un gallo desvaría,
reloj de medianoche. La grave luna amplía
las cosas, que se llenan de encantamientos mudos.

El lago azul de sueño, que ni una sombra empaña,
es como la conciencia pura de la montaña…
A ras del agua tersa, que riza con su aliento,

Albino, el pastor loco, quiere besar la luna.
En la huerta sonámbula vibra un canto de cuna…
Aúllan a los diablos los perros del convento.

NIGHT

Night in the mountain gazes with the widowed eyes
of a hapless doe watching over her young;
and, as if granted the gift of prophecy,
in an inspired dream the rough fields speak.

Three ecstatic poplars like sharp ghosts
scratch the landscape... A rooster raves on
like a midnight clock. The grave moon enlarges
things, which fill with mute spells.

The enchanted blue lake, untouched by shadow,
is like the mountain's pure conscience...
Mouth skimming the soft water curled by his breath,

Albino, the mad shepherd, tries to kiss the moon.
In the insomniac orchard a lullaby hums...
The convent's dogs howl at the demons.

EBRIEDAD

Apurando la cena de aceitunas y nueces,
Luth y Cloe se cambian una tersa caricia;
beben luego en el hoyo de la mano, tres veces,
el agua azul que el cielo dio a la estación propicia.

Del corpiño indiscreto, con ingenua malicia,
ella deja que alumbren púberas redondeces.
Y mientras Luth en éxtasis gusta sus embriagueces,
Cloe los bucles pálidos del amante acaricia.

Anochece. Una bruma violeta hace vagos
el aprisco y la torre, la montaña y los lagos.
Sofocados de dicha, de fragancias y trinos,

ella calla y apenas él suspírala: ¡Oh Cloe!
¡Mas de pronto se abrazan al sentir que un oboe
interpreta fielmente sus silencios divinos!

DRUNKENNESS

Finishing off their dinner of olives and nuts,
Luth and Chloe exchange soft caresses,
then drink thrice, from the hollow of their hands,
blue water rained by heaven on the auspicious season.

From the indiscreet bodice, with naïve cunning,
Chloe lets her pubescent curves peep out—
and, while an ecstatic Luth tastes their delights,
she strokes her lover's fair curly head.

Dusk falls. A violet haze blurs
sheepfold and tower, mountain and lakes.
Breathless with bliss, fragrances and chirps,

she is silent and he barely sighs to her: Oh Chloe!
But suddenly they embrace when they hear an oboe
faithfully interpreting their divine silences!

LA ZAMPOÑA

Lux no alisa el corpiño, ni presume en la moña;
duda y calla cruelmente, y en adustos hastíos
sus encantos se apagan con dolientes rocíos
y su alma en precoces desalientos otoña.

Job también hace tiempo receloso emponzoña
sus ariscos afectos con presuntos desvíos.
Y a la luna y durante los ocasos tardíos,
da en contar sus dolencias a la buena zampoña.

En casa, las amigas de Lux le hacen el santo,
la obsequian y la adulan… Bulle la danza, en tanto
Lux ríe. Su hermosura esa noche destella…

¡Mas de pronto se vuelve con nervioso desvelo,
la cabeza inclinada y los ojos al cielo,
pues ha oído que llora la zampoña por ella!

THE PANPIPE

Lux doesn't smooth her bodice or preen her bows,
but sorely doubts and grows silent—in sullen boredom
her charms fade under sorrowful dews
and her soul with early disappointment withers.

Job too has for some time jealously poisoned
his surly affections with her presumed fickleness—
and in the moonlight and through the late sunsets
recounts his woes to the good panpipe.

At home, Lux's girlfriends celebrate her name day,
shower her with presents and flattery... Dances buzz
while Lux laughs. Tonight her beauty shines...

But suddenly she turns with nervous watchfulness,
leaning her head with her eyes skyward,
for she hears the panpipe weeping for her!

EL CAMINO DE LAS LÁGRIMAS

Citándonos después de oscura ausencia
tu alma se derretía en largo lloro,
a causa de quién sabe qué tesoro
perdido para siempre en tu existencia.

Junto a los surtidores, la presencia
semidormida de la tarde de oro,
decíate lo mucho que te adoro
y cómo era de sorda mi existencia.

Pesando nuestra angustia y tu reproche,
toda mi alma se pobló de noche…
Y al estrecharte murmurando aquellas

remembranzas de dicha a que me amparo,
hallé un sendero matinal de estrellas
en tu falda ilusión de rosa claro.

THE PATH OF TEARS

Rendezvousing after a dark absence,
your soul melted into long weeping
because of who knows what treasure
forever lost to your life.

Beside the fountains and the drowsy
presence of the golden afternoon,
I told you how much I adored you
and how dull my existence had become.

Weighing our anguish and your reproach
my whole soul filled with night...
And as I held you, whispering those

memories of bliss in which I shelter,
I found a morning path of stars
in the pale pink illusion of your skirt.

AMOR SÁDICO

Ya no te amaba, sin dejar por eso
de amar la sombra de tu amor distante.
Ya no te amaba, y sin embargo el beso
de la repulsa nos unió un instante.

Agrio placer y bárbaro embeleso
crispó mi faz, me demudó el semblante.
Ya no te amaba, y me turbé, no obstante,
como una virgen en un bosque espeso.

Y ya perdida para siempre, al verte
anochecer en el eterno luto
—mudo el amor, el corazón inerte—,

huraño, atroz, inexorable, hirsuto…
¡jamás viví como en aquella muerte,
nunca te amé como en aquel minuto!

SADISTIC LOVE

I no longer loved you, but had not yet ceased
to love the shadow of your distant love.
I no longer loved you, and still the kiss
of aversion for a moment joined us.

Bitter pleasure and vicious fascination
contorted my face, turned my mien pale—
I no longer loved you, and yet was flustered
like a maiden inside a thick forest.

And seeing you, lost already and forever,
bedimmed in eternal mourning—
love fallen silent, the heart lifeless—,

and myself sullen, harsh, inexorable, cruel—
never did I live as under that death,
never did I love as I loved you then!

Alfredo Mario Ferreiro

VERSES WITH A FLYING ENGINE:
ALFREDO MARIO FERREIRO

Poet, critic, and journalist, Alfredo Mario Ferreiro was born and died in Montevideo (1899-1959). His only two poetry collections, *El hombre que se comió un autobús. Poemas con olor a nafta* (1927) and *Se ruega no dar la mano. Poemas profilácticos a base de imágenes esmeriladas* (1930), bear witness not only to a lively and irreverent attitude vis-à-vis language, but to an enduring "modern" and cosmopolitan inquisitiveness, which can be easily traced to Futurism, Ultraism and the rest of the programmatic movements that arrived in surges in Latin America as part of the so-called historical avant-garde of the early twentieth century.

The social and cultural context of both collections (to which we must add a prolific journalistic and prose output scattered among magazines and periodicals) was characterized by conformism and by a certain spiritual and intellectual torpor that ended up taking hold of the Uruguayan literary scene.[1] Nevertheless, in such a context, to strike a rebel attitude such as Ferreiro's—who launched his attacks from more than one trench, mainly that of *Cartel* magazine—cannot have been an easy task. He had to face a society "stupefied, corrupt in its power structures, and refusing to appreciate the whole of the national artistic production in all its extent" (Bravo 2013, 11).[2]

The renewing energy of his poems sought to shake the structures of the prevailing poetic language. Thus, his controversial and zingy style provoked a reaction that would challenge not only the way people wrote but also the way they read. This drive managed to successfully blend a cult of technological modernization and the noise of urban machinery—always brought on by novelty—with the nostalgic and contemplative sensitivity of local traditionalism. However, the most relevant element was not his ludic bravery, but the way he implemented this purpose with his pen. Through an original voice, he raised poetry writing to a category unusual in these parts. Ferreiro's literary project contributed "to the blurring of the borders between 'highbrow' and 'lowbrow' literature or between 'cultured' between 'highbrow' and 'lowbrow' literature or between 'cultured' and 'popular' poetry" (Rocca 13). This avant-garde and provocative gesture, which was not without a significant dose of humor and irony, can still be found in his pages and makes his works singular within Uruguayan and regional literature.

Recognition, however, was slow to arrive and is still in the process of establishment. The poems presented in this book follow this exciting path of dissemination.[3]

NOTES

[1] Regarding journalism, A.M.F. was a frequent contributor of articles to *La Razón* newspaper and to magazines aimed at diverse types of readers, such as *Vida Femenina* and *La Cruz del Sur*, among others. One specific text deserves highlighting from amidst such a richness of writings. In 1937, Ferreiro was appointed by the Uruguayan government to be a part of a delegation of local writers (headed by Enrique Amorim) entrusted with the mission of repatriating the remains of Horacio Quiroga, a writer from Salto who had died in Buenos Aires in February of that year. On the Argentine side, the accompanying delegation consisted of names such as Jorge Luis Borges and Ezequiel Martínez Estrada, among others. Almost twenty years after the event, Ferreiro wrote a deeply-felt and memorable chronicle of that journey, entitled "De cómo se nos perdió y encontramos a H. Quiroga" (Of How We Lost and Found H. Quiroga), valuable for posterity from the documentary and literary viewpoints, as he was the privileged witness of an event concerning one of Latin America's essential writers. The chronicle was published in *Marcha* (Montevideo, Nº 824, 825, and 827 respectively: August 3, 10 and 24, 1956).

[2] *Cartel: panorama mensual de literatura y arte* was co-directed by A.M.F. and Julio Sigüenza. Ten issues were published (1929-1930). Through the controversial pages of *Cartel*, Ferreiro "launched tough attacks on bureaucratized power [...], on apathy and political nepotism, on the petit-bourgeois status quo of the times and its scant sensitivity to anything that was not productive utilitarianism" (Ferreiro 8). *Cartel* also operated as a publishing house; the first edition of *Se ruega no dar la mano. Poemas profilácticos a base de imágenes esmeriladas* appeared in that publisher's Third Notebook (1930).

[3] From this revisionist viewpoint, it is enough to verify the scant survival of A.M.F.'s books in the years following the original publication. For example, four decades elapsed before *El hombre que se comió un autobús. Poemas con olor a nafta* (1927) was reprinted for the first time. In 1969 it was published as a notebook of the *Enciclopedia Uruguaya* (although without the original paratexts, and thus being arguably a different book). A third reprinting,

published on the basis of a copy corrected and prepared by the author in 1930, took a further thirty years to arrive. In 1998, Dr. Pablo Rocca rescued it for the "Socio Espectacular" series (Ed. Banda Oriental). The case of *Se ruega no dar la mano. Poemas profilácticos a base de imágenes esmeriladas* (1930) is even more remarkable: the first complete reissue took eighty years to arrive, in the form of a facsimile edition (2013) published through the joint effort of two Montevidean publishers, Yaugurú and Irrupciones.

POEMA DEL RASCACIELOS DE SALVO

El rascacielos de Salvo
es una jirafa de cemento armado
con la piel manchada de ventanas.

Una jirafa un poco aburrida
porque no han brotado palmeras de 100 metros.

Una jirafa empantanada en Andes y 18,
incapaz de cruzar la calle,
por miedo de que los autos
se le metan entre las patas y le hagan caer.

¿Qué idea de reposo daría un rascacielos
acostado en el suelo?

Con casi todas las ventanas cara al cielo.
Y desangrándose por las tuberías
del agua caliente
y de la refrigeración.

El rascacielos de Salvo
es la jirafa de cemento
que completa el zoológico edilicio
de Montevideo.

POEM OF THE SALVO HIGH-RISE[1]

The Salvo high-rise
is a reinforced concrete giraffe
with window-dappled fur.

A giraffe that is a little bored
because no 300-feet palm trees have sprouted.

A giraffe bogged down at Andes and 18,
unable to cross the street
for fear that cars will get
between its legs and trip it down.

What idea of repose would a high-rise
lying on the ground give?

With almost all its windows facing the sky.
And bleeding to death
along the hot water
and refrigeration pipes.

The Salvo high-rise
is the concrete giraffe
that completes the architectural zoo
of Montevideo.

---

[1] The Palacio Salvo, which opened its doors to the public in October 1928, and was originally a luxury hotel, remained for many years the tallest building in South America. It was built by the Salvo brothers, Italian immigrants to Uruguay who had become wealthy, at the intersection of 18 de Julio Avenue (familiarly known to Montevideans as "18") and Independencia Square, a few feet from the corner of Andes St. (see line 6). Despite its relative dilapidation and the impoverishment of its surroundings, it is still one of Montevideo's most emblematic and beautiful buildings (Translator's Note).

CASAS VIEJAS

La rueda de comadres de las casas viejas
se celebra de noche;
cuando todos duermen.

Cuando las casas jóvenes,
cansadas del ajetreo del día,
se han quedado dormidas
con los párpados metálicos bajos.

Las casas viejas, comadres del barrio,
charlan de estas cosas de ahora.
Critican los *bow windows*,
los pozos de luz,
el cemento,
los ascensores,
la calefacción.

Ellas se hacían la *toilette*
con pintura al aceite.

Odio de las casas viejas
para las casas nuevas.

Odio de la señora 1870
para la señorita 1927.

OLD HOUSES

The old houses' gossip gathering
is held at night,
when everybody sleeps.

When the young houses,
tired from the day's bustle,
have fallen asleep
with their metal eyelids closed,

these old houses, the neighborhood's gossips,
chat about this newfangled stuff.
They criticize the bow windows,
the light shafts,
the concrete,
the elevators,
the heating.

They used to do their toilette
with oil-based paint.

The hatred of old houses
for new houses—

the hatred of Mrs. 1870
for Miss 1927.

EL GRITO DE LAS COSAS[1]

Madre:
las cosas me gritan
que tus ojos posaron sobre ellas.

Aquí estuvieron,
aquí estuvieron sus miradas.

Y aquí,
y aquí también.

Y allá.

Madre:
Hay perfume de ojos tuyos
en el reflejo de recuerdos de las cosas.

Y yo las voy bordeando con los ojos,
como limitándolas: impidiendo   **O**
la terrible caída total de tu recuerd

---

[1] The use of a much larger font for the first and last letters in the poems from *Se ruega no dar la mano. Poemas profilácticos a base de imágenes esmeriladas* is a Ferreiro idiosyncrasy. We have tried to reproduce it here as faithfully as possible, in the originals as well as in the translations (Editor's Note).

THE SHOUT OF THINGS

Mother:
things are shouting at me
that your eyes alighted on them.

Here they were—
here were their gazes.

And here,
and here too.

And there.

Mother:
there is a scent of your eyes
in the reflection of memories of things.

And I skirt them with my eyes,
as if limiting them—preventing
the terrible total downfall of your memor **Y**

YO BIEN SÉ QUE NO HAS MUERTO

Yo bien sé que no has muerto.
No puedes haberte muerto.

Estarás escondida,
como a veces, en casa.

Cuando todos veníamos
y no estabas…

Entonces, te buscábamos,
y salíamos a la puerta.
Hasta que aparecías.

Madre:
Estoy en el vano
de un recuerdo esperando tu vuelta

I WELL KNOW YOU ARE NOT DEAD

I well know you are not dead.
You can't be dead.

You must be hiding,
as sometimes happened, at home.

When we all arrived
and you weren't there…

Then we searched for you
and looked out the door.
Until you appeared.

Mother:
I am at the threshold
of a memory, awaiting your returN

POEMAS DE LA CIUDAD LLOVIDA

I

Lluvia

La ciudad se ha encogido bajo la lluvia.
Apenas si, a lo lejos,
allá, junto a los murallones,
un barco envía una columnita de humo,
que es la única ofensa hacia arriba,
contra la lluvia.
La ciudad hubiese querido
disparar.
Guarecerse
debajo de aquel toldo
de nubes de allá lejos.
No ha podido.
Y, calándose de agua hasta los huesos de cemento,
soporta, resignada, la humorada del tiempO

II

Asfalto mojado

Un espejo borroso tirado entre las casas.
Puñaladas de luces.
Largas huellas de autos.
Dan ganas de salir con un secante
y dejar para siempre imborrable
la imagen invertida de las cosas
que están en el baúl transparente del asfaltO

POEMS OF THE RAINED-UPON CITY

I

Rain

The city has shrunk under the rain.
Only a faraway ship
there by the seafront walls
sends up a little column of smoke,
the sole upward-pointing offence
against the rain.
The city would have liked
to flee.
To take cover
under that awning
of clouds in the distance.
Hasn't been able to.
And, drenched to its concrete bones,
it resignedly bears the weather's whimS

II

Wet Asphalt

A blurry mirror lying between the houses.
The stabs of lights.
Long car tracks.
One would like to go out with blotting paper
and make forever indelible
the inverted images of things
inside asphalt's transparent trunK

III

Estrategia

Para que pase un largo regimiento de lluvia
se cierra el horizonte con un telón de nubeS

III

Strategy

So that a long regiment of rain may pass
the horizon is closed with a curtain of cloud**S**

PLAZUELA CON 4 BANCOS[1] Y UN APREMIANTE S.O.S.

(fragmento)

1er Banco

Siempre lo mismo

Siempre lo mismo!
Un día despertaré muerto.

Habré dejado el alma de mis versos
colgada en el perchero
de la entrada.

Y me saldré sin ella.
Y andaré por la calle
como un hombre.

¡Y sin alma!

Este poner un mismo númerO
en las rayas de siempre.
Este sumar renglones,
este "muy señor mío",
este final horrible
"saludo a Vd. atte."

¡Siempre lo mismo!
Un día despertaré muerto.
Colgada en el perchero
de la entrada

habré dejado el alma de mis versoS

---

[1] "Bancos" may be equally translated as "banks" or "benches". Ferreiro puns on both meanings, with the title hinting at benches in a square and the poems themselves clearly referring to banks (Translator's Note).

A SMALL SQUARE WITH 4 BANKS AND AN URGENT SOS (excerpt)

1st Bank

Always the Same

Alway**S**[2] the same!
One day I'll wake up dead.

I'll have left the soul of my verse
hanging from the coat rack
by the door.

And I'll leave without it.
And I'll walk in the streets
like a man.

And soulless!

This writing the same number
in the same blanks.
This adding of lines,
this "Dear Sir,"
these awful closing w**O**rds,
"I am, Sir, yours truly."

Always the same!
One day I'll wake up dead.
Hanging from the coat rack
by the door

I'll have left the soul of my ver**S**e.

---

[2] In the original poem, Ferreiro's larger font forms the word "SOS" In order to maintain this idiosyncrasy in the translation, we have had to apply the larger font to other words or parts of the relevant words (Translator's Note).

2do Banco

Máquinas de sumar

Las máquinas de sumar
toman tabaco de números.

Lo pican,
lo mascan,
lo ponen sobre la hojilla larga
del carretel perezoso;

y se hacen un tremendo cigarro,
encendido a ratos
por la chispa roja
de las sumas totales.

Cenizas de sumitas parciales;
y humo de intereses
para todos los clientes del BancO

3er Banco

Ventanillos

El público
no precisa argamasa
para convertirse en pared.

Delante del "guichet"
es un nervioso muro
del que salen las manos
de los emparedados vivos.
Unas manos con muecas,
prestidigitando dinero escabullidO

2nd Bank

Adding Machines

The adding machines
take number-tobacco.

They cut it,
chew it,
put it on the long blade
of the lazy reel;

and they roll a huge cigar,
lit every now and then
by the red ember
of total sums.

Ashes of little partial sums
and interest-smoke
for all the Bank's clientS

3rd Bank

Windows

The public
do not need mortar
to turn into a wall.

Before the *guichet*
they are a nervous wall
from which the hands
of the walled-alive stick out.
Grimacing hands
juggling filched moneY

y 4to Banco

Ascensores

Vienen subiendo,
como gimnastas;
manoteando las cuerdas;
palmeando los pestillos.

Traen la gente de abajo,
los que recién entran
al turbión de negocios.

Todos vienen gorjeando
cálculos
dentro de la jaul**A**

and 4th Bank

Elevators

Up they come,
like gymnasts—
pawing at the ropes,
patting the latches.

They bring people from down below,
those who have just joined
the maelstrom of business.

They all come up chirping
calculations
inside the cagE

LA MADRUGADA (fragmento)

Las veletas ignoran dónde quedará el viento.
Hay un ritmo de brisa que anda jugando a ciegas.
Tiemblan de frío las enredaderas.
Y un aletear de píos
sobre las arboledas.
La madrugada viene con un paso seguro,
remontando caminos empedrados de cielo.
A veces se detiene
para sacarse lunares de nubes.
Trae aplausos de alas
sobre lomos de pájaro.
Trae el ruido confuso de un despertar unánime.
Ya ha terminado el baile de los astros nocturnos.
Con su dedo largo, la luz hace cosquillas
en la piel azulada de una enorme laguna.
Así viene la aurora
a sorprender al hombre.
La noche se defiende con murallas de astros,
ráfagas de colores bombardean su cerco.

SMALL HOURS (excerpt)

The weather-vanes don't know where the wind may be.
There is a rhythm of breezes blindly playing.
Creepers shiver with cold.
And a fluttering of trills
upon the groves.
The small hours come with firm steps
up sky-cobbled roads,
stopping sometimes
to remove cloud moles.
They bring the applause of wings
on birdback.
They bring the confusing noise of unanimous awakening.
The dance of the night stars is over.
With its long finger, light tickles
the bluish skin of a huge lake.
Thus comes dawn
to surprise man.
Night defends itself with star walls;
gusts of color bombard its fence.

Susana Soca

A FOREIGN MEMORY:
SUSANA SOCA

Susana Soca (1906-1959) is a mysterious and strange figure in the Uruguayan literary landscape, thus the fitting title given to a recent biographical study: *Rara avis. Vida y obra de Susana Soca* (2012), a book we recommend to everyone who intends to better explore the career of this very peculiar writer.

It is difficult to accurately place Susana Soca, despite the more than fifty years elapsed since her tragic death in an airplane crash when she was still young. In spite of having her papers in front of us, her archive available, and the possibility of tracing her life story—as well as a greater attention from the critics who for so long neglected and ignored her, today Susana Soca continues to refuse categorization and will not be reduced to the sole name of "poet." She does not seem to ever have wanted that either.

The scion of an aristocratic family and daughter of the renowned Uruguayan physician and politician Francisco Soca, throughout her life Susana alternated between life in Uruguay and long sojourns in Paris, where she was well known. A cultural enabler, humanist, and patron of the arts, she was also a writer and editor of her own literary magazine. It is unjust to allocate any single role or interest to Soca, since her love for culture was greater than her dedication to creating a comprehensive literary opus. In this regard, critics have accused her of unevenness in the quality of her works, as if her poetry had not had the time to mature. Her early death might be the most obvious answer as to her truncated literary career, about which we can only speculate.

What we do know is that in France she was responsible for the cultural project *Cahiers de La Licorne* (1947-48), a somewhat Europeanized and elitist Franco-Spanish literary magazine (perhaps comparable with the editorial line of *Sur*, a contemporary Argentine magazine edited by Victoria Ocampo, with whom Soca held an elegant intellectual rivalry). In its Parisian stage, *Licorne* published only three issues, but Soca later continued it in Montevideo under the name *Entregas de La Licorne*, going on to publish ten issues between 1953 and 1961.

Thanks to her ongoing intercultural efforts and work, Soca managed to establish a priceless network of affinities between local/River Plate writers and European ones; this facilitated mutual connection and dissemination. As regards her own poetry, she prepared several anthologies, including *En un país de la memoria* (1959) and *Noche cerrada* (1962). Her great obsessions were the sea, memory, dreams, time, and poetry itself (her poetry, the inner score governing the poem), as well as the artist's creative will.

From the beyond, riding on her lyric unicorn, Soca continues to reflect on *ars poetica*, and introspectively challenges us with her delicate voice and enviable clarity of expression: "Whoever creates, in the difficult agreement between play and torment, makes music, but cannot listen to it: if he hears it, he cannot recognize it, because it appears to him as indefinitely alien. Only the presence of play and torment remain to him, from beginning to end. But others listen; sometimes music rises in them and, as always, this is the reality of poetry" (75).

SALMO DE LA NOCHE

Aquí la noche jadeante y baja. La que se muere y no habla.
Aquí la noche aferrada a la ceniza de la nieve. En las ciudades
prisioneras.

Hay que tocar la propia diestra para saber el camino del agua.
Y solo el agua divide el bosque negro de la ciudad inmóvil y
vendada que un encaje olvidado de luna serpentea.

Aquí la noche que no duerme. Y solamente encierra. Casi
sin albas la de mañanas tardías. Risa de colegiales corta un
instante el frío. Hasta que pasa en ella un silbido. Como a
través del vuelo de las palomas condenadas.

Solo la noche se inclina a desiertos parapetos. Un temblor de
siglos gira en las veletas agitadas por el cierzo. Y prolonga la
voz de los tambores ensordecidos.

Saltan sobre la nieve los centinelas como los osos cautivos.

En su prisión la bella aprende por vez primera a caminar en las
tinieblas. Y todavía nadie espera nada.

Mayo, 1941.

NIGHT PSALM

Here the panting and low night. The one that dies and does not speak. Here the night clinging to snow ash. In the prisoner cities.

One must touch one's own right hand to know the water's path. And only the water divides the black forest from the motionless and blindfolded city slithered by forgotten moon lace.

Here the sleepless night. The one that only encloses. Almost dawnless, a night of tardy mornings. Schoolchildren's laughter cutting the cold for an instant. Until a whistle passes through it. As through the flight of the doomed doves.

Only the night leans on deserted parapets. A tremor of centuries spins in the weathervanes shaken by the north wind, and prolongs the voice of the deafened drums.

The sentinels jump on the snow like captive bears.

In her prison, the fair one learns for the first time to walk in darkness. And still no one expects anything.

May 1941.

DESDOBLAMIENTO

Jardines quietos y nunca fijos cerca del mar
en el aire impecable
donde se mueve el lento olor de la resina
la hierba nueva asoma y ríe
al flanco de la antigua
en la tersura de las dos briznas entremezcladas.

A orillas de la sombra
del alto pino pulido al sol de mediodía
por el agua del alba
baila Analisa, sus pasos mide un simple ritmo.
Es reposado el movimiento
y sin peso el descanso de Analisa.

Sobre el verde cristal
el pie desnudo apenas turba la hierba lisa;
la niebla matinal
es todavía aire liviano
y un frescor de lavanda sube al cielo de abril.
Baila Analisa en un otoño como verano
ligeramente toca el tiempo en su tamboril.

Imito el gesto y el movimiento en el sosiego.
Los brazos forman un serpenteante rápido juego:
con ojos de paloma
ella lo ve y la mirada despacio asoma
hacia boscajes de ramas quietas y diferentes.
Y las palomas hunden su pico en las serpientes.

Toca el reposo como una mano la inmensa planta
de la tierra en otoño.
Punzante ahora es la dulzura

UNFOLDING

Still and never-fixed gardens near the sea
in the flawless air
where the slow scent of resin moves
the new grass sprouts and laughs
by the side of the old
in the softness of the two intermingled blades.

At the shadow's shore
of the tall pine polished in the midday sun
by daybreak's water
Annalisa dances, steps measured by simple rhythm.
Easeful is the movement
and weightless the rest of Annalisa.

Upon the green crystal
the naked foot barely disturbs the smooth grass;
the morning mist
is still light air
and a lavender freshness ascends to the April sky.
Annalisa dances in a summer-like autumn,
time lightly beating on her drum.

I imitate the gesture and movement in the calm.
The arms form a sinuous fast game:
with her dovelike eyes
she sees it and her gaze slowly turns
to thickets of quiet, different branches.
And doves sink their beaks into snakes.

The stillness touches like a hand the endless
plant of earth in autumn.
Poignant now is the sweetness

que no penetra y permanece al lado mío
en el pudor del aire.

Desde los manantiales
de las tinieblas la angustia mía desborda y sube,
hasta entregarme al nuevo día
como la punta de nueva espada.

Triste es lo cómico, eficaz el demonio ingenuo.
vuelve la reina de pie de cabra bajo la púrpura
a los viejos tinglados.

Soy la que sigue en la gramilla
los pasos de Analisa
soy la que gira sobre sí misma.

Si la más diestra se entorpeciera
si la más rápida se rezagara
aunque lo atroz tome el lugar del aire en mí,
sabría respirar.
Pero ya sigo hasta el final de la jornada
sin poder elegir.

that seeps not in, but remains by my side
in the air's modesty.

From the wellsprings of darkness
my anguish overflows and rises,
delivering me up to the new day
as to the tip of a new sword.

The funny becomes sad, the naïve demon is efficient.
The goat-footed queen returns under purple
to the old daises.

I am the one following Annalisa's
steps over the lawn,
I am the one who spins around.

If the deftest one turned clumsy,
if the fastest one fell behind,
even if the atrocious took the place of air in me,
I'd know how to breathe.
But I'm already on my way to day's end
with no choice.

A LAS SIETE LA LUNA

I

Vuelve a su infancia en medio de la escarcha
aquella que tomaba para sí
el esplendor de la reciente noche
y en transitoria casa de espejos recogía
el largo centelleo.
Avecindado a nuestros ojos cabe
alto y sin soledad el esplendor más solo.

Ayer, crecida luna, ajena desmesura
pesaba en las orillas, oscurecía el oro
para apartar la noche que nunca habla ni mira
y entre luces y luces
abre y cierra caminos para la experta sombra
y ella cedió su reino a la brillante noche
cedió su reino al reino de la luna.
La luna ya encendida en el ausente fuego,
mezcla el color de la cercana sangre
a los remotos vinos que lentamente bebe.

Al final abrumada de fulgores, inerte
cerca del día sueña con otra leve luna
pequeña, dura, aligerada y rápida.
Y despierta en los juegos que el alba no interrumpe.

THE MOON AT SEVEN

I

It returns to its childhood in the midst of frost,
the one who took for itself the splendor
of the recent night
and gathered in a transitory house of mirrors
the long scintillation.
High and without loneliness, the loneliest
splendor settles by our eyes.

Yesterday, waxing moon, alien excess
weighed on the shores, darkened the gold
to draw aside the night that never speaks or looks
and between lights and lights
opens and closes roads to the skillful shadow
that has yielded its kingdom to the bright night,
yielded its kingdom to the moon's kingdom.
The moon already lit in absent fire
mixes the color of near blood
to the remote wines it slowly drinks.

At last, overwhelmed by brightness, inert,
near day it dreams of another slight moon,
small, hard, lightened and fast.
And wakes up to games unhindered by daybreak.

II

Es otra luna y su canto
una canción de alborada
es el alba de la luna
más que la luna del alba.
Hija del solo esplendor
de la noche en la mañana,
un instante suspendida
como la nube que baja,
lenta nieve de verano
en mitad de la montaña.
Esta es la luna de otoño
liviana, breve y lavada
como la piel de las hojas.
Puro perfil se adelanta
ágil en medio del día
camina sobre la escarcha
precoz del rígido cielo
entreabre una senda blanca,
como en los tupidos bosques
de la tierra, angosta y blanda.
Allí comienza lo blanco
y súbitamente acaba,
en el alba de la luna
más que en la luna del alba.

II

It's another moon and its song
a sunrise song
it's the dawn of the moon
more than the moon of the dawn.
Daughter of the lone splendor
of night in the morning,
suspended for an instant
like the lowering cloud,
slow summer snow
in the middle of the mountain.
This is the autumn moon
light, brief and washed
like the skin of leaves.
A pure profile going nimbly
forward in the midst of day
walking on the early
frost of the rigid sky
opening a white path
as in the thick forests
of the earth, narrow and soft.
There the white begins
and suddenly ends,
in the dawn of the moon
more than the moon of the dawn.

ALTA LA NOCHE

I

Junto a mis ojos, la noche erguida
alta estriada de blanco,
no la redonda pura certera oscuridad.
Sólo la noche llena de signos
donde vacilan los cautelosos
lúcidos animales.
Junto a mis ojos, alta la noche
llena de objetos apenas suyos
que fueron nuestros: nada de ellos
ha sido retirado.

No la fluida pura certera oscuridad
que en la obediencia sirve
a una noche que está muy lejos
y nunca se equivoca,
sin otra luz que la primera estrella fija,
y de nosotros nada.

Junto a mis ojos la noche breve
contradictoria llena de juegos y de boscajes
y de pie en ella, sobre algún mar
sin rumor y sin peso,
en el reflejo veo la sombra
del día que no encuentro.

TALL IS THE NIGHT

I

Beside my eyes, the erect night
tall and white-striated,
not the round pure unerring darkness.
Only the night full of signs
where the cautious lucid animals
hesitate.
Beside my eyes, tall is the night
full of objects barely its own
that once were ours: nothing of them
has been withdrawn.

Not the fluid pure unerring darkness
which obediently serves
a night that is very far away
and never wrong,
with no light but the fixed first star,
and nothing of us.

Beside my eyes the brief contradictory
night full of games and of groves
and standing on it, above some sea
without rumor or weight,
I see in reflection the shadow
of the day I cannot find.

II

Vasta y ligera
alegría que ignoro
como si yo la conociera
la adivino en el oro
fugitivo, y el dejo
que un instante resbala
sobre apagado espejo,
rectamente señala
hacia algún mismo punto
en el lúcido centro
del día que no encuentro
allí veo el trasunto
del largo día
entero en la alegría
o no es mar ni lugar
solamente la vía
para poder llegar
despacio a la alegría
ligera y sin reproche.
Algo brilla a destiempo
en mitad de la noche
como si fuera el día,
o en el entero tiempo
de la noche y el día
es sombra de alegría.

II

Vast and light
joy that I ignore
as if I knew it
I divine it in the fleeing
gold, and the trace
that in a moment slides
over a dull mirror
straightly points
to some identical spot
in the lucid middle
of the day I cannot find
there I see the likeness
of the long day
whole in joy
or neither sea nor place
only the way
to arrive slowly
at happiness
light and without reproach.
Something shines untimely
in the middle of the night
as if it were day,
or in the whole time
of night and day
is joy's shadow.

NOCHE Y CRUZ

Por el camino de una noche mía
anuladora exacta,
entro sin gestos, sin golpear en vano,
en la noche de todos.

Como ninguna pródiga en modos antes de morir,
cuando en secreto el áloe da renovados zumos
para llegar a innumerables bocas,
cuando el nocturno pecho dentro de mí jadea,
la cruz de la noche entra en la cruz de mis manos
sobrellevada a tientas y de pie.
Es la noche sin tregua, la que busca cien muertos
para aprender hasta qué extremo un solo
agonizante puede respirar.

Cuando persigue el hombre sin cesar al hombre
la misma trampa sirve para el uno y el otro
la misma ausente mano
hace cortar el cuello del lobo y de la tórtola.
Y la rutina ordena
con más rigor que la pasión difunta.
Cuando persigue el hombre en cada sitio al hombre,
a los unos da muertes que no serían la suya,
al uno quita el alma, al otro sepultura.
Una metralla ciega hasta en los muertos cava
y la mano de un niño cuelga de frescos olmos.

En súbito tumulto
se incendia la noche desde adentro.
Se reduce el antiguo lugar para la sombra,
como muros y troncos se parten las tinieblas.
Desaparecen ellas, las casas y los bosques.

NIGHT AND CROSS

Along the path of a night of mine,
precise obliterator,
I walk without gestures, without vain knocking,
into everyone's night.

Matchlessly prodigal in manners before dying,
when the aloe plant secretly gives renewed juices
to countless mouths,
when the nocturnal breast pants inside me,
the night's cross enters the cross of my hands,
borne by groping and standing.
It is the relentless night that seeks a hundred dead
to learn the extent to which one single
dying man can breathe.

When man ceaselessly pursues man
the same trap serves for one and the other
the same absent hand orders
to cut the wolf's throat and the turtle's.
And routine's decrees
are harsher than defunct passion's.
When man everywhere pursues man,
to some he metes out deaths that wouldn't have been theirs,
one he robs of his soul, the other of his grave.
Blind shrapnel carves even the dead
and a child's hand hangs from cool elm trees.

In sudden uproar
night catches fire from within.
The ancient place for shadow is reduced,
the darkness is cleft like walls and trunks.
It disappears with the houses and forests.

Una noche con ojos abiertos para siempre
ha de seguir en busca de los perdidos párpados.
Ahora es el tumulto
y la cruz de la noche silenciosa,
en la cruz de las manos.

A night with its eyes open forever
must continue seeking for the lost eyelids.
Now it is the uproar
and the cross of silent night
in the cross of the hands.

Líber Falco

AN INTIMATE SONG TO CONSCIOUSNESS:
LÍBER FALCO

Verses full of sentiment (but not sentimental), verses that resort to simplicity (while refusing to take the "easy way"), verses whose music is even today connected to the heart and ear of Uruguayans, poetry readers or otherwise. The work of Líber Falco (1906-1955) has certain very particular features that make it the ideal door through which to step into poetry. Because Falco has the timeless ability to whisper low into our conscience, with depth and emotion, about issues that concern us all—death, loneliness, anguish and love—and has, above all, the ability to portray, as no one else can, the spiritual and nostalgic landscape of the Montevidean soul, through a frank, compassionate, and quiet voice that only a born poet could deploy in such few verses without tainting them with affectation.

With regard to his literary context, Falco was a part of the so-called "Generation of '45" or "Critical Generation," although only marginally so: he was a secondary character in that movement. He led a modest life, working at humble jobs that included those of a baker and a hairdresser. He was an outsider to the intelligentsia of his time, despite having contributed to some magazines and newspapers and being close friends with several literati, such as Arturo Sergio Visca, Mario Arregui, Anderssen Banchero, Domingo L. Bordoli, and Carlos Martínez Moreno.[1]

His lack of interest in or distance from the literary environment did not prevent him from creating and developing a style of his own, faithful to his local or urban—one could even say "neighborhood-centered"—approach. It is thus that we have before us a brief but touching corpus: *Cometas sobre los muros* (1940), *Equis andacalles* (1942), *Días y noches* (1946) and *Tiempo y tiempo* (1956), the latter, a posthumous collected works that fortunately continues to be a kind host to the many generations who read its pages thanks to constant reeditions.

The poetry of Líber Falco does not offer readers a set of orderly verses that may be analyzed formally or dissected by the tireless aesthetes of language. No; Falco's poetry pursues a higher aim: to reach out to the reader in search of a brotherly connection. In other words, the expressional strength of Falco's poems lies in the spiritual communion they offer the reader. The generous possibility of opening up to such a pact—one of the main features of his poetic voice—enables human and emotional identification with his writing. That is why Falco is not merely a Uruguayan poet, but a poet we may genuinely call "our own."

NOTES

[1] The "Generation of '45" was one of the most creative and rigorous in Uruguayan and Latin American literature. It boasted of such writers as Carlos Martínez Moreno, Emir Rodríguez Monegal, Ángel Rama, Mario Arregui, Carlos Real de Azúa, Carlos Maggi, Alfredo Gravina, Mario Benedetti, Idea Vilariño, Ida Vitale, Juan Carlos Onetti, Washington Lockhart, Domingo L. Bordoli, Arturo Sergio Visca, José Pedro Díaz, and many others. They converged around some relevant publications, such as the weekly *Marcha* and the magazines *Número* and *Asir*, to name only the most important. This was the first literary generation that was fully aware of itself as a group and proclaimed itself as such, being part of a corrosive and anti-establishment attitude. "With the Generation of '45 there came an unheard-of expansion of literary criticism, so much so that before 1960, when some of its members started publishing fiction and other genres in book form, the movement was accused of being abusively and invasively hypercritical. This judgment was not only premature but also untrue, and came for the most part from offended interests. [...] In addition, that need to exercise criticism had another reason: the absence of criticism of the previous generations [as was the case with the so-called "Centennial Generation"—so named because it flourished around 1930, the centennial of the first Uruguayan Constitution—with some exceptions such as Gervasio Guillot Muñoz and Roberto Ibáñez]" (Paganini, 1969).

EXTRAÑA COMPAÑÍA

A Arturo Sergio Visca

Porque estoy solo a veces,
porque sin Dios estoy, sin nada,
ella viene y muestra su rostro y ríe
con su risa helada.
Viene, golpea en mis rodillas,
huye la tierra entonces
y todo acaba sin memoria, y nada.

Sin embargo, con ella a mi costado
yo amé la vida, las cosas todas;
lo que viene y lo que va.
Yo amé las calles donde,
ebrio como un marino,
secretamente fui de su brazo.

Y a cada instante, siempre, en cada instante
con ella a mi costado,
del mundo todo, de mis hermanos
lejano y triste me despedía.

Mas tocaba a veces la luz del día.
Con ella a mi costado,
ebrio de tantas cosas que el amor nombraba,
como a una fruta
tocaba a veces la luz del día.

Y era de noche a veces y estaba solo,
con ella y solo;
pero la muerte calla
cuando el amor la ciñe a su costado.

STRANGE COMPANY

For Arturo Sergio Visca

Because I am alone sometimes,
because I am without God, without anything,
she comes and shows her face and laughs
her icy laugh.
She comes, beats on my knees,
then the earth flees
and everything ends without memory, and nothing.

And yet with her by my side
I loved life, things all;
what comes and what goes.
I loved the streets where,
drunk as a sailor,
I secretly linked arms with her.

And each moment, always, every moment
with her by my side,
of the world all, of my brothers,
distant and sad I took my farewell.

But I sometimes touched the light of day.
With her by my side,
drunk with so many things that love named,
like a fruit
sometimes I touched the light of day.

And it was night sometimes and I was alone,
with her and alone;
but death is silent
when love presses her to his[1] side.

---

[1] In Spanish, the noun for death ("muerte") is feminine, while the
noun for love ("amor") is masculine (Translator's Note).

Oh triste, oh dulce tiempo cuando acaso
velaba Dios desde muy lejos.

Mas hoy ha de venir y ha de encontrarme solo,
ya para siempre desasido y solo.

Oh sad, oh sweet time when perhaps
God watched over from afar.

But today shall come and find me alone,
now forever unanchored and alone.

DESPEDIDA

A mis compañeros y compañeras de Corrección y Talleres
del diario Acción

La vida es como un trompo, compañeros.
La vida gira como todo gira,
y tiene colores como los del cielo.
La vida es un juguete, compañeros.

A trabajar jugamos muchos años,
a estar tristes o alegres, mucho tiempo.
La vida es lo poco y lo mucho que tenemos;
la moneda del pobre, compañeros.

A gastarla jugamos muchos años
entre risas, trabajos y canciones.
Así vivimos días y compartimos noches.
Mas, se acerca el invierno que esperó tantos años.

Cuando el Sol se levanta despertando la vida
y penetra humedades y delirios nocturnos,
¡cómo quisiera, de nuevo, estar junto a vosotros
con mi antigua moneda brillando entre las manos!

Mas se acerca el invierno que esperó tantos años.
Adiós, adiós, adiós, os saluda un hermano
que gastó su moneda de un tiempo ya pasado.
Adiós, ya se acerca el invierno que esperó tanto años.

FAREWELL

For my fellow-workers at the Correction and Press Department of Acción *newspaper*

Life is like a spinning top, my friends.
Life spins as everything spins,
and has colors like the sky's.
Life is a toy, my friends.

We played work for many years,
played sad or happy for a long time.
Life is what little and much we have—
the currency of the poor, my friends.

At spending it we played many years
amidst laughter, toil and song.
Thus lived we the days, shared the nights.
But winter, who waited for so long, is near.

When the sun comes up waking life,
penetrating the dampness and night's frenzies,
how I wish I were with you again,
with my old coin shining in my hand!

But winter, who waited for so long, is near.
Goodbye, goodbye, goodbye, says to you the brother
who has spent his coin from a time already past.
Goodbye, the winter who waited for so long is now near.

LO QUE FUE

Vienes por un camino
que mi memoria sabe,
y me detengo entonces
indagándote el rostro.
Mas ¡ah!, ya no es posible
siquiera, no es posible
detenerte un instante.

Todo está muerto, y muerto
el tiempo en que ha vivido.
Yo mismo temo, a veces,
que nada haya existido;
que mi memoria mienta,
que cada vez y siempre
—puesto que yo he cambiado—
cambie, lo que he perdido.

WHAT WAS

You come along a road
that my memory knows,
and then I stop
to query your face.
But oh! it's no longer even
possible, not possible
to stop you for a moment.

Everything is dead, and dead
the time in which it has lived.
I myself fear sometimes
that nothing has existed—
that my memory lies,
that each and every time
(since I am changed)
what I have lost too may change.

LUNA

Tan perfecta y blanca.
¡Tan alta!
Tan lejana y blanca.

Lejos de la muerte,
y de la vida lejos.
Lejos de los llantos.
De las risas, lejos.
¡Tanto!

No sabe esta luna
cómo todo es triste.
Cómo es bello el mundo
y la misma muerte acaso,
acaso, es volver sin irse.

Sola arriba, sola.
Tan perfecta y blanca.
¡Tan alta!
¡Tan lejos de todo!

Nada arriba, nada.
Ella sola y nada.

MOON

So perfect and white.
So high!
So far away and white.

Far away from death,
and from life far away.
Far away from tears.
From laughter, far away.
So far!

It doesn't know, this moon,
how everything is sad.
How the world is fair
and death itself may perhaps,
may be, perhaps, a returning without leaving.

Alone up there, alone.
So perfect and white.
So high!
So far away from it all!

Nothing up there, nothing.
It alone and nothing.

AHORA

Dame tu mano y vamos
entre la tarde, tristes,
a recordar los días
que se fueron.

Aquella mi pobre casa
donde en dura pobreza
bebimos la dulzura
aquélla ya no existe.

Eras alegre entonces
y a veces eras triste.

Mas, dame tu mano ahora
oh, amor, dame tu mano y vamos
a recordar siquiera,
lo que ya no existe.

NOW

Give me your hand and let's go
through the afternoon, sad,
remember the days
that have gone.

That, my poor house,
where in hard poverty
we drank sweetness—
that is no more.

You were happy then,
and you were sad sometimes.

But give me your hand now,
oh love, give me your hand and let's go
remember at least
what is no more.

APUNTE

Cantan allá abajo.
Unos muchachos cantan
mientras la Luna arriba,
como una blanca flor nocturna
derrama su esplendor sobre la Tierra.

Cantan allá abajo
y el canto sube.
Entre la noche sube
como un rezo.

NOTE

They're singing down there.
Some young men are singing
while the Moon above
like a white night flower
spills its splendour on Earth.

They're singing down there
and the song rises up.
Amidst the night it rises up
like a prayer.

DESEO

A M. M.

A veces quisiera uno
sin días que lo nombren,
perderse, camino hacia el olvido.
Porque para qué alumbra el día
si tantas muecas de los hombres,
como un mapa de angustias
e indescifrables signos
de mariposas muertas,
giran sin término.

También quisiera uno,
luego de tanto y tanto
amor al aire,
que un árbol se recline
a bebernos la frente.

WISH

For M. M.

Sometimes one would wish
—free of days that call one's name—
to lose oneself towards oblivion.
Because what is daylight for—
when so many human grimaces,
like a map of anguish
and indecipherable signs
of dead butterflies,
are spinning endlessly.

And one would also wish
after such and so much
love of air
that a tree would bend forward
to drink from our foreheads.

EL ABISMO

Estoy debajo de mis sueños.
Ya ni estrellas ni pájaros nocturnos
levantarán mi canto.

Puente de plata y oro es el amor.

Amada, tú eras el único asidero
pero yo he mirado el abismo
donde ondula (libre de nosotros)
el limo de mis sueños y tus sueños.

Desde entonces ¡ah!
qué solo estoy en la tierra.
Y tú, qué sola.
No lo sabes y disuelves tus lágrimas en risas.
Desde entonces,
cuando apoyo mi frente
en el tibio regazo de tu seno,
algo quiero olvidar que no conozco todavía.
Y crece mi ternura para ahuyentar el miedo.

Lejana erra mi alma
y en sus flancos llueve la tristeza.
Deja que te llore y que me llore allá…

THE ABYSS

I am under my dreams.
No stars, no night birds shall
lift up my song any more.

A bridge of gold and silver is love.

Beloved, you were all I could hold on to,
but I have looked into the abyss
where the slime of my dreams and yours
ripples, bereft of us.

Since then, how lonely I am on earth!
And you, how alone.
You don't know—your tears dissolve in laughter.
Since then, when I lean my forehead
on your warm breast,
I want to forget something I don't yet know.
And my tenderness swells to chase away the fear.

Far away errs my soul,
and on its flanks a sad rain is beating.
Let me mourn you and myself there...

HERRERITA

Blasfemo, trashumante y señorial
iba el bohemio bebiendo el aire
por las calles.

La pipa un periscopio cosmogónico,
el sombrero ladeado y con desgano,
iba el poeta retando el hambre
por las calles.

—Hermanos, estamos hechos
de incontables hambres— dijo
y se fue el poeta
por la más larga,
definitiva calle.

HERRERITA

Blasphemous, errant and stately
went the bohemian drinking air
along the streets.

His pipe a cosmic periscope,
hat at a listless angle,
went the poet daring hunger
along the streets.

"Brothers, we are made
of countless hungers," said
the poet, and vanished
down the longest
street and final.

En un baldío
cinco muchachos juegan a la pelota.
Un hombre pasa.
Lleva una carretilla. Pasa.
Un aire suave
abanica el rostro de la tarde.
A lo lejos, allá…
los palacios del Centro
muestran su espalda al Sol.
La tarde se va.
Lleva un aire de doncella defraudada.

En un baldío,
cinco muchachos juegan a la pelota.
Montevideo vive.
No sueña. No espera nada.
Vive.
Lejos suena una bocina.
Qué triste es todo.
Y sin embargo, qué bello es verlo,
mirarlo, oírlo y verlo.

In a vacant lot
five boys play soccer.
A man passes by
pushing a wheelbarrow. Passes.
A soft breeze fans the afternoon's face.
In the distance, the downtown palaces
turn their backs on the sun.
The afternoon goes,
with the air of a jilted maiden.

In a vacant lot,
five boys play soccer.
Montevideo lives.
Doesn't dream. Doesn't hope.
Lives.
A car honk is heard in the distance.
How sad everything is,
and yet, how fine to see it—
to watch, to hear, to see it.

Pedro Piccatto

SWEET POETRY OF A BITTER ANGEL:
PEDRO PICCATTO

The life of Pedro Piccatto (1908–1944) did not resemble that of other disgraced poets, loaded with unhappy love affairs, nor may his experience be compared—unfortunately—to that of a "normal" person. He was physically disabled as a consequence of a childhood accident that left him with a hump for the rest of his life. This "mark" of destiny not only conditioned his life experience and relationship with his environment, but also influenced the expressional content of his writing. His was a lonely, intense, different soul.

As happens with many other artists, Piccatto's personal life (thanks to the construction and dissemination of urban myths) is better known than his works. In this he is similar to Susana Soca, Roberto de las Carreras, or Federico Ferrando, to mention a few examples. Indeed, sometimes a man's reality can be stronger and more mysterious than any of his creations.[1]

El ángel amargo (1937) and *Anticipaciones* (1944) were his only two books. The latter was posthumously financed by writer friends, including Líber Falco and Mario Arregui. In 2008, the contents of both books were collected in *Las anticipaciones del ángel amargo* (Ed. Yaugurú), at last giving us access to Pedro Piccatto's collected works. His is not an urban poetry, steeped into his social context or ideological or political elements. On the contrary, it is an emotional, introspective, suggestive, and magical poetry, which engages in a dialogue with the poet's inner world and uses the outer world's imagery for bringing down to earth words, reflection, and desire. The poetic universe of Piccatto is built through a simple language that is nonetheless deep and rich, as well as lively and lucid. His speech is sometimes guided by a strong rational drive, but starts tapping before long into a metaphysical, even religious current.

Although the scope of his themes is limited, this should not be viewed as a negative aspect, as it is precisely the paucity of subjects that creates a virtuoso concentration in the central issues of his poetry: he knows the borders of his kingdom thoroughly, and keeps all the keys to himself. The figure of the angelic, the idea of transcendence, gardens, and seas are recurring metaphors in Piccatto's texts. Flowers, greatly relevant to his poetry and often regarded from a philosophical viewpoint in their change and transformation, are in the midst of a dark landscape and always possessed of a special luminousness. The presence of the mother, another relevant subject, is the shelter and support of life—she is the poet's protector and creative muse.

From the formal viewpoint, Piccatto's poems break with hendecasyllables, rhyme, and the traditional canon in general. His is a kind of succinct and brief free verse where expressive force is deployed to the utmost. He has a natural ability for inventing neologisms that conjure a strange prolongation or duration effect, such as "sangral," "campanal" or "corazonal"[2]. His originality was also reflected in the graphic area, since he proposes peculiar poem layouts and verse orders. Through this unpredictability, Piccatto exercises melodic and rhythmical control of his poems, as if the notes of each of this "bitter angel's" songs were a part of a greater score, half earthly, half divine.

NOTES

[1] For more information on this author and other little-known Uruguayan artists, we recommend the project *Los pájaros ocultos* (2011), a cycle of HD documentaries directed by writer and producer Juan Pablo Pedemonte and aimed at the dissemination of Uruguayan artists (José Parrilla, Pedro Piccatto, Marosa di Giorgio, and Jorge Meretta, among others). All of them, in the opinion of specialized critics, have in common the fact that they created a high-quality, undervalued body of work that for different reasons remains hidden or neglected. The purpose of *Los pájaros ocultos* is to reveal their work in order to promote culture. The documentaries were created within a project that also included introductions and tributes to the artists in different events. The documentary about Pedro Piccatto may be viewed here: www.lospajarosocultos.com/piccatto/largo.php.

[2] In the contexts where they appear, these words may be tentatively translated as "bloodplace" or perhaps "blood hours" (as in "book of hours") in the case of "sangral;" the more straightforward "bell-like" in the case of "campanal," which is used as an adjective; and "heartplace" in the case of "corazonal." Only the latter appears in our selection. (Translator's Note).

JARDÍN Y MAR (fragmento)

I

Floral,
marina fantasía
este poema…
esta fuga tenaz hacia otra cosa,
este feliz delirio de agua y flor.

¡Corazonal!
                    ¡Sin par!

II

Un mar de hierbas blancas,
de arena en flor,
un mar de hojas azules,
de rosales cautivos,
                    perseguidos…

¡Un mar soñado!
                    ¡Un solo mar!
                              ¡Mi mar!

III

Del mar,
del mar,
de su jardín de porcelana y miedo
la flor del mar
                    nos llega.

GARDEN AND SEA (excerpt)

I

Floral,
marine fantasy
this poem...
this stubborn fleeing towards something else,
this happy delirium of water and flower.

Heartplace!
          Peerless!

II

A sea of white grass,
of sand in bloom,
a sea of blue leaves,
of captive rosebushes
               pursued...

A dreamed sea!
               A single sea!
                   My sea!

III

From the sea,
from the sea,
from its garden of porcelain and fear
the seaflower
           reaches us.

Corona de la brisa.
Espejismo del pájaro.

¡La flor del mar!

Ay cómo sueña
su aroma de cristal
su aroma fija
su corazón preso en el agua.

IV

Un sitio blanco
y un latido mudo.
Muerta
la rosa mía.

Donde ella muere,
madre,
no hay que cruzar pisando fuerte.

Lo sabe el viento,
el pájaro,
esa sima sin grietas del sexo y la amapola,
la luz,
la mariposa…
¡Y el mar!
¡El mar!
Lo sabe el mar que nunca vio una rosa.

Breeze-crown.
        Bird-mirage.

The seaflower!

        Oh how it dreams
        its crystal scent
        its scent fixes
        its captive heart in the water.

IV

A white place
        and a mute heartbeat.
        Dead
            my rose.

Where she dies,
        mother,
        one must not tread heavily.

The wind knows,
the birds,
that creviceless abyss of sex and poppy,
the light,
the butterfly...
        And the sea!
               The sea!
The sea knows, who's never seen a rose.

XII

El agua es bella aunque no tenga flores.
Lo piensa el mar pero su sueño es otro.

Vivo andar de amapolas perseguidas
sueña que le retiene una sirena.

Y cada ola quebrándose en la espuma
le hace gozar la rosa azul deseada.

XIII

Su luz,
jazmín del aire.

Oceánica,
celeste,
reflejada en la arena,
esta luna del mar es otra luna
que la de mi jardín.

¡Luna-mar, luna-mar, luna-jardín!
¡Tiene que haber dos lunas para mí!

XII

The water is fair although it has no flowers.
Thus thinks the sea, but its dream is different.

A strong gait of pursued poppies,
it dreams it is held back by a mermaid.

And each wave breaking into foam
makes it enjoy the wished-for blue rose.

XIII

Its light,
jasmine of the air.

Oceanic,
sky-blue,
reflected on the sand,
this sea-moon is different
from my garden's moon.

Moon-sea, moon-sea, moon-garden!
There must be two moons for me!

AZUL EN SOMBRA (fragmento)

I

Yo tenía
          un descanso.

¿Bajo qué corazón
bajo qué pie
          pude perderlo?

II

Muerta
          la mariposa.
          Crucificada
                    sobre la cruz de un vuelo.

Ahora tiene su cielo entre las hojas de un libro.

De un libro
que no habla de mariposas
ni de muertes.

BLUE IN SHADOW (excerpt)

I

I had
        rest.

Under which heart
under which foot
            could I have lost it?

II

Dead,
        the butterfly.
        Crucified
            on the cross of flight.

Now she has her heaven between the pages of a book.

Of a book
that speaks not of butterflies
or deaths.

III

Cortina, esencia, el corazón
en la alta rosa va creciendo.

Hay que buscar en la alta rosa
lo que alabamos en secreto.

Lo que aún no dio la luz del seno
hay que buscarlo en la alta rosa.

Hay que buscar en la alta rosa
lo que ignoramos desde el ángel.

Lo que perdemos bajo el ángel
hay que buscarlo en la alta rosa.

No hay que buscar en la alta rosa
lo que perdemos sin el ángel.

VI

¡Cuánto esplendor de dalia asesinado
y cuánta voz de carne sin enaguas!

¡Cuánta abeja que quiso ser estrella
y cuánto corazón contra la piedra!

¡Cuánto albor de sustancia desgarrada
y cuánta brasa azul en la madera!

¡Cuánta carne con alas por adentro
y cuánto girasol bajo la lluvia!

¡Cuánto asco de sábana ultrajada
y cuánta pana helada entre dos besos!

III

Curtain, essence, the heart
in the tall rose is growing.

We have to seek in the tall rose
what we praise in secret.

What the light of the womb has not yet yielded
we have to seek in the tall rose.

We have to seek in the tall rose
what we have ignored since the angel.

What we lose under the angel
we have to seek in the tall rose.

We must not seek in the tall rose
what we lose without the angel.

VI

How much dahlia-splendor murdered
and how much voice of flesh without petticoats!

How much bee that wanted to be star
and how much heart against the stone!

How much dawn of torn substance
and how much blue ember in the wood!

How much flesh with wings on the inside
and how much sunflower in the rain!

How much disgust of affronted bedsheets
and how much nerve lost between two kisses!

SIETE POEMAS

I

Suelto este canto:
alguna que otra rosa
entre pantano
y piedra.

II

Hoy
una fácil revelación,
ayer
una virtud difícil, ardua,
mañana…

¡mañana
ya lo dirán la flor
el guijarro
la estrella
y mi dolor!...

                                 Secreto
en estuche de brisa
naciendo
de lo exacto del mundo,
                                     mi infinito.

SEVEN POEMS

I

I release this song:
some rose or other
between bog
and stone.

II

Today
an easy revelation,
yesterday
a difficult, arduous virtue,
tomorrow—

tomorrow
the flower,
the pebble,
the star
and my pain will tell!
     Secret
in the breeze's jewel case
arising
from the world's exactness,
       my infinite.

III

¡Qué mal! qué mal
se explican mis heridas.
Y eso que para ello sólo tienen
la sangre y la palabra.

Sólo
la sangre y la palabra.

IV

Se nos iba
la rosa…

Yo la detuve con mi dulce miedo
y mi blanca amargura.

¡Pero sólo un instante!...

Entre un coro de luz
cada pétalo
vivía de milagro.

Y próximo a caer
se sonreía…

Hay sonrisas en la rosa
casi tan mías como mi muerte…

                                    ¡la muerte!

III

How badly! How badly
my wounds explain themselves,
despite having for that purpose
only the blood and the word.

Only
the blood and the word.

IV

It was leaving us,
the rose...

I stopped it with my sweet fear,
with my white bitterness.

But for a moment only!

Amidst a chorus of light
every petal
lived by miracle.

And when about to drop
it smiled...

There are smiles in the rose
almost as mine as my death...

                        death!

V

Me lo dijo una amiga
y yo lo escribo:
a la azucena
no le gusta que le cuenten
lo que oye el abanico antes del beso.

A la amapola, sí.

VI

Al mar,
junto al difícil beso de una perla,
le nace una sirena.

Melodía
de agua color y nube;
pensamiento
de caracol
      y arena.

Al mar,
     le robo,
               tul de jardín,
                       su sueño.

Yo le robo
          su sueño
             su delirio:

ay la amapola de sensual campana
y la rosa de místico sosiego
y la azucena de soleada nieve
y la rama del árbol bajo el pájaro
y lo infinito del aroma dándose.

V

A friend told me
and I'm writing it:
white lilies
don't like being told
what the fan hears before the kiss.

Poppies, on the other hand, do.

VI

From the sea,
beside the difficult kiss of a pearl,
a mermaid is born.

Melody
of color water and cloud;
thought
of conch
       and sand.

From the sea
          I steal

              —garden tulle—

                      its dream,

I steal from it
          its dream
              its delirium:

ah the sensual bell-shaped poppy
and the mystically peaceful rose
and the sunny-snowed lily
and the tree bough under the bird,
and the endlessness of scent giving itself.

VII

Para morir no necesito verte.
Para vivir sí que lo necesito
que necesito verte,
uva estrellada.

VII

To die, I don't need to see you.
But to live I do need it—
need to see you,
star-spangled grape.

MIEL ESTÉRIL (fragmento)

I

Celeste,
        herida,

                y sin violencia,
como nacida cuando muere el último
pétalo de una rosa,
quisiera yo que fuera
esta canción.

II

Entre azafrán y naranja
era el crepúsculo
un espumón del iris.

Un zarzal de dulzura
en donde se apagaban
impotentes
los odios de los hombres.

Donde se daban cita
las finas amapolas del deleite
y la blanca palabra de la luna.

… Me acuerdo bien:
        cruzaron
        tres parejas de pájaros.

Vuelo de mirasoles en hilera.

BARREN HONEY (excerpt)

I

Sky-blue,
            wounded,

                        and without violence,
as if born when a rose's last
petal dies,
I would like this song
to be.

II

Between saffron and orange
was the dusk
the iris' rising foam.

A bramble of sweetness
where men's hatreds
were quenched
to powerlessness.

Where the fine poppies
of delight rendezvoused
with the moon's white word.

… I remember well:
            three pairs
            of birds flew across.

A flight of sunflowers in a row.

Pulso de Dios
       latían
       zambullidos de luz
             como incitando.

La libertad en el ala
       y en el alma.

V

¡Dos mariposas blancas
persiguiéndose!

¡Dos llamitas de nieve
sostenidas!

¡Dos estrellas movibles
persiguiéndose!

¡Dos mariposas blancas
liberadas!

¡Parejita de sueños!...

       Musical
    toque de luna de los aires.

The pulse of God
    they throbbed
    drenched in light
     as if provoking.

Freedom in the wing
    and in the soul.

V

Two white butterflies
chasing each other!

Two little sustained
flames of snow!

Two moveable stars
chasing each other!

Two white butterflies
released!

Little dream pair!

    Musical
   touch of air moon.

Humberto Megget

A LIGHT THAT WILL NOT SLEEP:
HUMBERTO MEGGET

The poetry of Humberto Megget (1926-1951) was not, and is not, very well known in Uruguay. This statement, which applies mainly to poets outside the traditional canon (Pedro Piccatto being another clear example) or not often read or consulted in libraries by most readers, should not be in any way surprising. Not even having been a part of the so-called "Generation of '45" or "Critical Generation" could grant Megget a more prominent place in our literature. However, more than sixty years after his death, we are here discussing his literary work, not just out of critical revisionism but also because of his quality as a writer.

Due to his early death (he was barely 24 when he succumbed to tuberculosis), Megget did not leave a copious body of work. Indeed, *Nuevo sol partido* (1949) was the only book published during his lifetime. This slim collection of poems was twice reprinted, as *Nuevo sol partido* (1952) and *Nuevo sol partido y otros poemas* (1965); the latter edition was prepared by the famous poet and fellow '45er, Idea Vilariño, who unearthed unpublished poems not included in the previous editions. Still later, Megget's works were collected in *Humberto Megget. Obra completa: poesía y prosa* (1991), an edition prepared by scholar Pablo Rocca.

Idea Vilariño, in her introduction to the 1965 edition, refers to the need to acquaint readers with the context of Megget's poems, in order to understand "what Megget himself may not have fully known: the extent to which his poetry was different, brave and original in the dull poetry scene of our forlorn, busy and seminal 1940s" (12). Intuitive and ludic, rigorous but at the same time experimental, Megget's poetry was an original alternative to his fellow poets' rationality, including that of Vilariño herself.

His expressional path was nourished by different sources: he harnessed Surrealism's, Creationism's, and Ultraism's experiences, due to the strong influence of another "strange" poet, José Parrilla— like him, Uruguayan and neglected. Megget's renewing and neo-avant-garde spirit led him to explore the terrain of performance poetry, and he also edited the short-lived magazine *Sin zona* (December 1947), where he published his first relevant poems.

As regards to style, readers may immediately feel the freshness of his imagery, the reflexive strength of his longer works and the songlike tone changes of his shorter ones, as well as the tireless iterative, rhythmical and hypnotical patterns of most of his poems. Humberto Megget's voice continues to ring in the magical corners of his "new sun," and, despite the time elapsed, has no intention of fading.

Ay ay cómo me duelen
estos retazos de flores en mis manos
ay ay cómo las dejo
con sus ojitos de tierra
ay ay cómo me duele
esta pierna que es derecha
esta pierna que es izquierda
ay ay cómo las dejo
en el camino escondidas
entre la hierba y el fresco
ay ay cómo me duelen
tantas piedras y colinas
entre tu cuerpo y mi cuerpo.

Oh oh how they hurt
these pieces of flowers in my hands
oh oh how I leave them
with their little earth eyes
oh oh how it hurts
this leg that is right
this leg that is left
oh oh how I leave them
by the roadside hidden
between the grass and the cool
oh oh how they hurt
so many stones and hills
between your body and my body.

tengo ganas de risas raquel
tengo ganas de ir al cine a ver aquella película
ganas de ver las rosas y no ver las rosas
tengo ganas de tomar el café con leche
y beber
beber
beber
beber
beber
beber aquello y esto
y lo que tú das
y lo que yo ofrezco
ganas de ir y no ver aquella película
tengo ganas de ti y de aquél
pero más que de ti y de aquél
tengo ganas de coca y de raquel

i feel like laughing raquel
i feel like going to the cinema to see that movie
like seeing the roses and not seeing the roses
i feel like having coffee and milk
and drinking
drinking
drinking
drinking
drinking
drinking that and this
and what you give
and what i offer
i feel like going and not seeing that movie
i feel like having you and that one
but more than having you and that one
i feel like having coke and raquel

YO MI SOBRETODO VERDE

Yo mi sobretodo verde
yo mi cáscara de nuez
yo mi gota de agua
mi río
mi árbol
yo corcel galopando en una orilla
brazos del viento descansando en los árboles
me acostaré tal vez quién sabe en dónde
en el polvo o en un mosquito
para ser el grito de un cocodrilo
o las manos abrazadas al fondo de un río
yo en una hoja caído
en una gota de agua envuelto
para no volver nunca
puedo seguir mucho tiempo deambulando en los aires
tal vez tenga la forma invisible de un microbio
o quizá esté en el aletear del vuelo de una mosca
hay tanto
tanto espacio para volar mi cuerpo inútil
tanto manantial donde poner mis pies frágiles
tantos redondeles blancos en los ojos cerrados
que en mi inconsciente voluntad de estar, así
no estoy solo.

I MY GREEN OVERCOAT

I my green overcoat
I my nutshell
I my drop of water
my river
my tree
I a steed galloping along a shore
arms of the wind resting on the trees
will lie down maybe who knows where
on the dust or on a mosquito
to be the scream of a crocodile
or the hands hugging the bottom of a river
I fallen on a leaf
in a drop of water wrapped
never to return
can go on wandering the air for a long time
maybe have the invisible shape of a microbe
or be in the flapping of a fly's wings
there is so much
so much space where to fly my useless body
so many springs where to put my brittle feet
so many white circles in the closed eyes
that in my unconscious desire to be, I'm thus
not alone.

TENGO EL SUEÑO

Tengo el sueño
y el viento
y el traste aparte
la comodidad de verme todos los días
y el oído de siempre oyendo mis palabras
tengo también el cuerpo que es un arco
esperando lanzarse sobre algo
y en los movimientos que hace mi cabeza
tengo todo un paisaje de cosas diarias
el fusil
el alba
mi medalla
tengo la voluntad de verme fácil
pero también el cierre de no entregarme
y entretener el tengo de mil cosas
tengo
tengo
tengo
tengo este sonido de tengo con gusto a guitarras.

I HAVE THE DREAM

I have the dream
and the wind
and the backside aside
the comfort of seeing myself each day
and the usual ear hearing my words
I also have this body like a bow
waiting to spring upon something
and in the movements of my head
I have a whole landscape of daily things
the rifle
the dawn
my medal
I have the will to see myself easily
but also the closing-down of not surrendering
and entertaining the I have of a thousand things
I have
I have
I have
I have this I have sound that tastes of guitars.

Va a dormirse una luz sobre mi frente
una luz en el cuarto este que toco
en el cuarto este de aguas que no bebo
de hojas mal impresas
y de estufas calientes.
Va a dormirse una luz
una luz que se estira en varias líneas
que no tiene
ni boca
ni estornudos
ni dedos para pies
ni pies sin dedos
sobre mis dientes mordiendo una manzana.
Va a dormirse una luz
hasta mañana.

A light is about to fall asleep on my forehead
a light in this room that I touch
in this room of waters I don't drink
of misprinted pages
and of hot stoves.
A light is about to fall asleep
a light that stretches over several lines
and has no
mouth   `
or sneezes
or toes for the feet
or feet without toes
on my teeth that bite into an apple.
A light is about to fall asleep
until tomorrow.

Cuando tú estés dispuesta
comeremos
un pedazo de manzana en automóvil
y cuando regresemos
de una higuera recogeremos higos
y alimentaremos a gorriones vagabundos
cuando tú estés dispuesta
se sobrentiende
nos entretendremos en aprender el idioma de lombrices
en dibujar con carbones caravanas de hormigas
y luego subiremos como por un tronco hacia la montaña
y plantaremos la primera flor para sonrisa de los aviadores.
Cuando tú estés dispuesta haremos tantas cosas
nos pondremos a descansar bajo las palmeras
y a descubrir cómo se hacen el amor los grillos
luego correremos con nuestras alforjas al mar
y las llenaremos de espumas
que agitaremos en el espacio para que formen sobre nuestros cuerpos techos
que cobijarán el secreto de nuestras representaciones nocturnas
siempre
claro está
cuando tú estés dispuesta.

When you are willing
we will eat
a piece of apple in the car
and when we get back
from a fig tree we will pick figs
and feed wandering sparrows
when you are willing—
it is understood—
we will amuse ourselves by learning the language of earthworms
by making charcoal drawings of ant caravans
and then we will climb towards the mountain as if up a tree trunk
and plant the first flower for the aviators' smiles.
When you are willing we'll do so many things
lie down to rest under the palm trees
and discover how crickets make love to each other
then we'll run to the sea with our knapsacks
and fill them with froth
which we'll shake in the air so that it will be a roof over our bodies
sheltering the secret of our nocturnal performances
provided
of course
that you are willing.

Cómo se ensancha este mundo
cuando tú niña caminas.
Tienes los ojos de troncos
y tus dedos son bordados
del agua de las colinas.

How this world widens
when you my girl walk.
You have eyes like trunks
and your fingers are embroidered
from the water of the hills.

Yo tenía una voz
botas de niño recién puestas
bombacha campesina más que rota
herida en las rodillas
era una voz que dominaba
a gigantes pequeños de juguete
que hiciérame anidar entre gorriones
y madurar la mente entre los hombres
que cortaban los árboles y el césped.
Yo tenía una voz tan pequeña
que hacía con ella collarcitos
y ataba tantas cosas a su corazón de trigo
que un día hasta a una niña tuvo presa
a una niña de ojos de dedales
con pestañas de fibra de los linos
a una niña de niña más que niña
que tomando a mi voz entre sus dedos
la convirtió en palabra de los ríos
y me quedé sin ella.

I had a voice
a child's boots newly put on
gaucho pants more than torn
wounded at the knees
it was a voice that ruled over
little toy giants
that made me nest among the sparrows
and my mind mature among the men
who cut the trees and the grass.
I had a voice so small
that I wove little necklaces out of it
and tied so many things to its heart of wheat
that one day even a girl was its prisoner
a girl with thimble eyes
with linen fiber eyelashes
a girl as a girl more than girl
who taking my voice between her fingers
turned it into the rivers' word
and left me without it.

BIBLIOGRAPHY USED IN THE INTRODUCTIONS

Amengual, Claudia. *Rara avis. Vida y obra de Susana Soca*. Montevideo: Taurus, 2012.

Bravo, Luis. *Voz y palabra. Historia transversal de la poesía uruguaya 1950-1973*. Montevideo: Estuario, 2012.

-----. Introduction. *Se ruega no dar la mano. Poemas profilácticos a base de imágenes esmeriladas*. By Alfredo Mario Ferreiro. Montevideo: "Rescate" series, Yaugurú/Irrupciones, 2013.

Courtoisie, Rafael. *Antología esencial. La poesía del siglo XX en Uruguay*. Madrid: Visor libros, 2011.

Falco, Líber. *Tiempo y Tiempo*. Prologue by Heber Raviolo. Montevideo: Banda Oriental, 2006.

Ferreiro, Alfredo Mario. *El hombre que se comió un autobús. Poemas con olor a nafta*. Ed. Pablo Rocca. Montevideo: Colección "Socio Espectacular", Banda Oriental, 1998.

-----. *Se ruega no dar la mano. Poemas profilácticos a base de imágenes esmeriladas*. Montevideo: "Rescate" series, Yaugurú/Irrupciones, 2013.

-----. "De cómo se nos perdió y encontramos a H. Quiroga." Montevideo: *Marcha*. Nº 824, 825, and 827 respectively: Aug. 3, 10, and 24, 1956.

Herrera y Reissig, Julio. *Poesía completa y prosas*. Ed. Ángeles Estévez. Madrid: Galaxia Gutenberg, 1999.

-----. *Tratado de la imbecilidad del país, por el sistema de Herbert Spencer*. Ed. Aldo Mazzucchelli. Montevideo: Taurus, 2006.

Megget, Humberto. *Nuevo sol partido y otros poemas*. Ed. Idea Vilariño. Montevideo: Banda Oriental, 1965.

-----. *Obra completa. Poesía y Prosa.* Ed. Pablo Rocca. Montevideo: Banda Oriental, 1991.

Mirza, Roger. *Julio Herrera y Reissig. Antología y estudio crítico.* Montevideo: Arca, 1975.

Paganini, Alberto. "Los críticos del 45." *Capítulo Oriental. La historia de la literatura uruguaya.* N° 35, Montevideo: Centro Editor de América Latina, 1969.

Pedemonte, Juan Pablo. *Los pájaros ocultos.* Tremendo Films, Fondos concursables para la cultura, MEC, 2011. Documentaries on Uruguayan writers and artists José Parrilla, Pedro Piccatto, Miguel Ángel Tosi, Clever Lara, Enrique Estrázulas, Álvaro Figueredo, Marosa di Giorgio, Alfredo Fressia, Lucio Muniz and Jorge Meretta. www.lospajarosocultos.com

Piccatto, Pedro. *Las anticipaciones del ángel amargo. Obra completa de Pedro Piccatto.* Montevideo: "Rescate" series, Yaugurú, 2008.

Rocca, Pablo (Ed.). *Alfredo Mario Ferreiro: una vanguardia que no se rinde.* Montevideo: Comisión Sectorial de Investigación Científica, UdelaR, 2009.

Soca, Susana. *Noche cerrada en un país de la memoria.* Montevideo: "Rescate" series, Yaugurú, 2010.

BIBLIOGRAPHY USED IN
THE TRANSLATIONS

For Herrera y Reissig:

Mirza, Roger. *Julio Herrera y Reissig. Antología y estudio crítico.*
  Montevideo: Arca, 1975.
Herrera y Reissig, Julio. *Poesía completa y prosa selecta.*
  Caracas: Biblioteca Ayacucho, 1978.

For Ferreiro:

Ferreiro, Alfredo Mario. *El hombre que se comió un autobús. Poemas con
  olor a nafta.* Montevideo: Ediciones de la Banda Oriental,
  1998.
-----. *Se ruega no dar la mano. Poemas profilácticos a base de imágenes
  esmeriladas.* Montevideo: Yaugurú / Irrupciones, 2013.

For Soca:

Soca, Susana. *Noche cerrada en un país de la memoria.* Montevideo:
  Yaugurú, 2010.

For Falco:

Falco, Líber. *Tiempo y tiempo.* Montevideo: Ediciones Asir, 1956.

For Megget:

Megget, Humberto. *Nuevo sol partido y otros poemas.* Ed. Idea Vilariño.
  Montevideo: Banda Oriental, 1965.

For Piccatto:

Piccatto, Pedro. *Las anticipaciones del ángel amargo.* Montevideo:
  Yaugurú, 2008.

ACKNOWLEDGMENTS

Thanks are due to the editors of the publications where the following poems, or earlier versions or parts of them, first appeared:

Coal City Review (USA): "Sadistic Love" (Julio Herrera y Reissig); "Poems of the Rained-Upon City" (Alfredo Mario Ferreiro); "The Abyss" and "Herrerita" (Líber Falco); "Garden and Sea" (Pedro Piccatto); as well as Falco's "Farewell" in my chapbook, *Midnight at the Law Firm*, published by Coal City Press.

The Journal (UK): "In a vacant lot…" (Líber Falco).

The Louisville Review (USA): "Wish" (Líber Falco).

Magma (UK): "Garden and Sea" (Pedro Piccatto); "i feel like laughing raquel" (Humberto Megget).

Modern Poetry in Translation (UK): "Strange Company," "What Was," and "Now" (Líber Falco).

spoKe (USA): "In a vacant lot…" (Líber Falco).

I wish to thank Laura Cesarco Eglin of Veliz Books for her generosity and editorial skills, and for encouraging my project of disseminating the work of fellow Uruguayans who deserve wider recognition—a concern which she shares—; and Gerardo Ferreira for his comprehensive and engaging introductions.

This book is dedicated with love to my daughter and niece, small but enthusiastic book lovers and part of the next generation of Uruguayan readers.

Laura Chalar was born in Montevideo, Uruguay, where she trained as a lawyer and obtained her postgraduate degree in International Commercial Arbitration. She is the author of two collections of short stories, two poetry collections, and an English-language chapbook of poetry, *Midnight at the Law Firm* (Coal City Press, 2015). She has also published numerous translations from and into Spanish, among them works by Jane Austen and Jules Supervielle, and Uruguayan poetry dossiers in different magazines. A translation into Spanish of Mary Wollstonecraft's *Thoughts on the Education of Daughters* and a children's story based on poems by Líber Falco are forthcoming. Chalar is the recipient of several literary awards, and she is also a Pushcart Prize nominee. Her first short-story collection in English, *The Guardian Angel of Lawyers,* is forthcoming.

Gerardo Ferreira, BA in Literature (FHCE, University of Uruguay), is a writer and cultural journalist. He has published the poetry collections *Imagina el desierto* (Ed. Simbiosis, 2009) and *La sensación es un lugar* (Irrupciones, 2013). With researcher Andrés González, he worked on the project *Horacio Quiroga: contexto de un crítico cinematográfico. Diálogos con "Caras y Caretas" y "Fray Mocho" (1918-1931)*, published in *Cuadernos de la Biblioteca Nacional* (Uruguayan Ministry of Education and Culture, 2014). He has written for several Uruguayan media, *la diaria*, *El Boulevard,* and *Lento* among others. Besides literature, he enjoys film, TV series, and real life as well.